ooh! History

of

Space

SQueeaK

Sally Kindberg
and Tracey Turner

BLOOMSBURY

Contents

Wheee!

IN THE BEGINNING...

Who knows? There are plenty of theories though...

absolutely NOTHING

or

BIFF BUMP BASH

A parallel Universe bumped into ours.

Or, an all-powerful GOD created everything.
(There are many different versions of him/her/it.)

Oooh, I know!
TWIDDLE TWIDDLE

Woooo

Krk!

or

A cosmic egg hatched.

God being born

Nnn

or maybe

The SKYWOMAN fell on to a GIANT TORTOISE.

Oi!

Ooh, sorry!

Then (probably)...

1

BIG BANG THEORY

In 1927, a priest called GEORGE LEMAÎTRE was studying astronomy...

Now just about everyone accepts BIG BANG theory. It says...

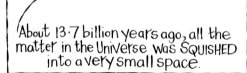

About 13.7 billion years ago, all the matter in the Universe was SQUISHED into a very small space.

It was incredibly HOT

and incredibly DENSE. Lots of stuff—EVERYTHING actually—packed in here

Then it exploded, E-X-P-A-N-D-I-N-G outwards...

And then, about 300,000 years after the Big Bang...

The Universe cooled down enough for ATOMS to form.

The nuclei were a bit useless on their own, so they met up with electrons and became ATOMS.

Hi... I'm an ELECTRON.

And I'm irresistibly drawn to you.

We give things structure. Without us there wouldn't be any THINGS at all!

Ooh... I'd go weak at the knees if I had any!

And we allow LIGHT to travel. Without us everything would be DARK.

GULP!

I just love all this attention!

Now we're an ATOM!

EVERYTHING is made of atoms. Without atoms the Universe would be clouds of particles. and nothing else.

An ancient Greek called DEMOCRITUS was the first person to think about atoms.

Hmm...

Erm...

Everything's made up of really titchy things

...which are the smallest things there are!

I know! I'll call them άτομα *

*atoms

Apart from hydrogen and helium, nothing else existed until millions of years later...

A Star is born...

The Universe carried on COOLING, and GRAVITY pulled the hydrogen and helium closer together

WHOOSH WHOOSH

...causing NUCLEAR REACTIONS

...which created the first STARS (giant balls of burning GAS) ...and so the first GALAXIES were born.

There are about 100 BILLION stars in the MILKY WAY.

There are HUNDREDS of BILLIONS of galaxies in the Universe

Some galaxies are SPIRALS, some are ELLIPSES, and some are just BLOBS.

The Milky Way, our galaxy, is a very attractive spiral.

I'm a BLOB and proud of it!

The Sun

Long after the Big Bang, a huge cloud of hydrogen and helium was whizzing through space...

Whooshy WHOOSH

Dust and stuff in here too, made from other STARS.

Suddenly...

WHUMP!!!!

it was squished into a DISC.

Hmm... maybe because of a nearby supernova?

From the huge disc of gases our SUN was formed...

Like other stars, the Sun is a giant ball of burning hydrogen gas... It is the closest star to Earth.

Inside the Sun, NUCLEAR REACTIONS turn 240 tonnes of hydrogen into heat and light EVERY MINUTE

At its core, the temperature is around 15 MILLION° C!

Whew!!

Hmm? hmm?

Why? Why?

The Sun is more than a MILLION MILLION times bigger than the Earth.

Great gas bubbles pop out of the CORONA during SUN STORMS.

BLIP BLOP

The corona extends millions of kilometres out into space from the surface of the Sun. It's nowhere near as bright as the surface, yet it's millions of degrees HOTTER This puzzles scientists.

And, eventually, there was ...

OUR SOLAR SYSTEM

Dwarf planets

The planets and moons that ORBIT our Sun formed 46 billion years ago.

Neptune

Uranus

Saturn

Hitch-hiking not recommended.

Jupiter

Asteroid Belt

Mars

Earth

Venus

Even though it speeds along, light still takes A DAY to cross our solar system.

Mercury

The Sun

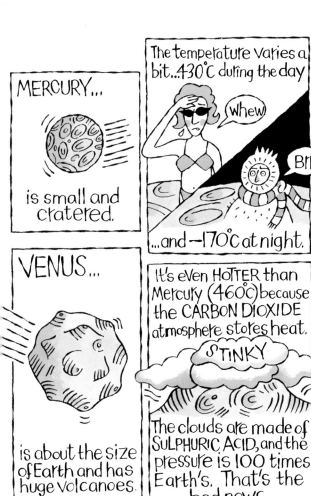

MERCURY... is small and cratered.

The temperature varies a bit...430°C during the day (Whew) ...and -170°C at night. Brr...

The atmosphere is very thin. Radiation from the Sun is INTENSE! SIZZLE SIZZLE

VENUS... is about the size of Earth and has huge volcanoes.

It's even HOTTER than Mercury (460°C) because the CARBON DIOXIDE atmosphere stores heat. STINKY

The clouds are made of SULPHURIC ACID, and the pressure is 100 times Earth's. That's the bad news...

The good news is that it can be your birthday and Christmas EVERY DAY of the year... creak creak

as Venus spins slowly, so a DAY is longer than a YEAR on Earth.

EARTH... All mod cons. Lots of WATER. PEOPLE and STUFF. (more on that later)

MARS

Deimos

CANYONS

Phobus

has the highest MOUNTAINS in the solar system.

People thought there might be LIFE on Mars...

Look! There's a canal system...

I hope the MARTIANS are friendly!

If there ever was life, it looked like this...

simple BACTERIA

and died out millions of years ago.

Little do you know, foolish earthlings!

Nng!

A·S·T·E·R·O·I·D   B·E·L·T

JUPITER...

GREAT RED SPOT

Jupiter's a GAS GIANT—as are Saturn, Uranus and Neptune

is absolutely HUGE... twice as HEAVY as all the other planets put together.

Jupiter is a giant ball of LIQUID and GAS (though there's a core of solid hydrogen).

SQUOOOOSH

An enormous HURRICANE has been raging away on Jupiter for more than 300 years (this is Jupiter's famous Great Red Spot).

SATURN...

RINGS of ICE

is also very BIG.

lots of MOONS

Saturn is another GASSY planet. It's very cold (−176°C) and even windier than Jupiter.

Brrr!

WHOOSH

One of Saturn's moons, TITAN, is bigger than the planet Mercury.

URANUS...

lots of MOONS

Very stinky

is four times the size of Earth, colder than Saturn, and covered in liquid METHANE.

Uranus wasn't discovered until 1780.

Hello! I'm WILLIAM HERSCHEL.

Ooh!

Find out about that on page 50.

One of its moons, PUCK, has three craters called BOGLE, LOB and BUTZ.

NEPTUNE...

raging storms

WHOOSH WHOOSH

is rather like Uranus but it has 2,000 km/h WINDS.

Neptune wasn't discovered until 1846. It takes so long to orbit the Sun that a year on Neptune is 165 EARTH YEARS.

Read how on page 51.

I'm JOHANN GALLE. I found it!

There used to be a ninth planet called PLUTO, but it's been demoted to a dwarf planet because it's so SMALL.

Sniff sniff

PLANET EARTH

Whizzes through space, spinning around once every 24 hours or so...

Attractive blue colour because WATER covers nearly 75% of surface

Giant ball of solid NICKEL-IRON at centre

Earth's CRUST is a thin layer of ROCK

Thick layer of gases covers the planet - the ATMOSPHERE

Water is essential for life on Earth.

Nice day!

The atmosphere FILTERS some of the Sun's harmful RADIATION. It's also useful for BREATHING.

Magnetic field

The metal ball makes the Earth like a giant MAGNET. This is useful because it deflects harmful particles from the Sun.

Sections of the Earth's crust grind against each other, causing EARTHQUAKES and VOLCANOES.

CREAK   BIFF   BASH   BLIP

And even creating MOUNTAINS and CONTINENTS (which takes a while).

As well as orbiting around the Sun ONCE a year...

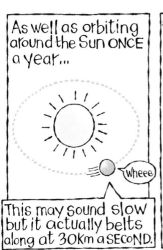

Wheee

This may sound slow but it actually belts along at 30km a SECOND.

the Earth also spins on its AXIS...

Twirl twirl

Equator

which is TILTED.

That's why we have SEASONS.

WINTER

SUMMER

The NORTHERN HEMISPHERE is angled AWAY from the Sun in WINTER, and TOWARDS the Sun in SUMMER. And it's the other way round for the SOUTHERN HEMISPHERE.

A few million years after the Earth formed...

BASH

SCRUNCH

DEBRIS

Something huge crashed into it.

debris forms MOON

Our Moon reflects light, which is handy at night...

Hnnn.

And it's so romantic!

and makes the Moon look as if it changes shape while it orbits the Earth.

Back on Earth...

Waiter, there's a single-cell organism in my soup!

And we were nosier than the dinosaurs...

Prehistoric People Look Up and Get Curious

People started wondering...

Hmm

Scritch scratch

Ooh...

Er....

The Sun gives us light and heat.

We don't like the cold and dark.

We certainly don't!

Hnn hnn

Nng nng

And the Sun and Moon divide time in chunks.

See you at next full Moon then.

Righty-ho.

The changes of the Sun, Moon and stars show us when to plant and harvest.

Yum!

People had interesting ideas about
what MIGHT be going on UP THERE...

But the Babylonians were the REAL smartypants...

THE ANCIENT BABYLONIANS

They also thought up names for the constellations...

Constellations

Ancient peoples saw pictures amongst the brightest stars and started to give them names. Babylonian astronomers saw a SCORPION...

We're the Maya of South America.

And even though we've never met the Babylonians, we've decided it looks like a scorpion too...

Yeah!

But the Maya disagreed about other constellations.

That's GEMINI, the Twins.

No it's not—anyone can see it's a PECCARY!

NB A peccary is a creature very like a pig.

What you see in the night sky depends on the time of year and where you are on Earth. And whether or not it's cloudy.

There are some stars I can't see because they're only visible from the Southern hemisphere.

And there are some I can't see. But there are quite a few we can BOTH see.

Ancient peoples weren't only interested
in space by night...

Ancient Chinese Ideas

This is what happens in a SOLAR ECLIPSE

Moon blocks Sun's light

SUN

EARTH

MOON

and a LUNAR ECLIPSE.

SUN

EARTH

MOON

Earth's shadow falls on Moon

Solar eclipses are particularly dramatic.

Aargh

YOWL

Urk

The first record of a total eclipse of the Sun was in 2136 BC in China.

Pull yourself together and write it down!

Nnnn!

Unfortunately, solar eclipses were seen as a very bad omen in China.

Oh no, a dragon's devouring the Sun!

No, a dog's eating it!

Whichever way you look at it, this can't be good!

WHIMPER

So Chinese astronomers/astrologers spent a lot of time trying to foretell when they would occur.

We'll all need to hide under our beds a week next Tuesday.

SIGH

The ancient Egyptians had
some groovy ideas too...

Ancient Egyptian Ideas

Every sunrise, the ancient EGYPTIAN god RE was born.

Gurgle

By midday he was an adult.

By evening, he was old.

Creak

Behave!

Sss!

I want to stop you on your journey!

And at night he travelled through the underworld.

Many other Egyptian gods were seen in the stars.

Look, there's OSIRIS, god of the dead.

So it is!

The MILKY WAY is the goddess NUT giving birth to Re!

I say!

The night sky was divided into groups of STAR GODS travelling in boats.

This is fun!

Ancient Egyptian priests were also astronomers.

We can PREDICT things...

like the annual flooding of the NILE.

The flood was important, which made the priests important too.

The flood is coming!

It happens after the bright star SIRIUS rises before the Sun.

Isn't he clever!

From around 2000 BC, Egyptian astronomers recognised FIVE planets (which we know as Mercury, Venus, Mars, Jupiter and Saturn).

SBG is bright tonight

Is that good or bad?

*Sbg was an ancient Egyptian name for Mercury.

Some Egyptian buildings were aligned with the stars.

But the ancient Greeks had some REALLY good ideas...

DARK AGE ASTRONOMERS

In EUROPE, nobody bothered thinking about space much

All that maths and stuff...

Who cares?

Anyone for a rampage?

Learned works of civilised world go up in smoke.

At ALEXANDRIA, the great library was burned down.

In INDIA, BRAHMAGUPTA had some clever thoughts...

The Earth is a moving sphere.

The Moon is illuminated by the sun.

Hmm

In POLYNESIA, people had become star experts to help them navigate thousands of kilometres by sea.

Follow that star!

In NORTH AMERICA, the ANASAZI people painted the bright supernova explosion they'd observed in the sky.

Good heavens!

And in CHINA...

We noticed this too!

37

Copernicus

Copernicus's universe...

But Copernicus's calculations couldn't explain the way the planets moved...

Kepler, Brahe (and Moose)

Galileo

GALILEO GALILEI was an Italian astronomer, mathematician and philosopher.

And physicist actually.

Among other things, he improved the design of the newly invented TELESCOPE*

Oooh!

*His design and lenses meant he could MAGNIFY by 30 times.

And discovered the moons of JUPITER.

Golly...

Four of them orbiting Jupiter. It's a bit like the planets going round the Sun.

(We now know Jupiter has loads of moons... about 60... but we do have better telescopes.)

Galileo also discovered that the planet VENUS has phases...

Caused by the Sun shining on it as Venus orbits.

This helps prove that the Sun's at the centre, not the Earth.

And that SATURN has something a bit STRANGE going on...

Hmm... Saturn appears to have EARS!

Unfortunately...

The Earth goes round the Sun and these observations seem to... um... prove it!

Gnash! Nnng!

In 1635, Galileo was condemned by the church and sentenced to house arrest. Seven years later...

Urk

Huygens

Telescopes

Hubble has taken the most detailed pictures of the most distant objects in the Universe...

Pillars of Creation in EAGLE NEBULA

SOMBRERO GALAXY

Cosmic Pearl round an exploding star

CAT'S EYE NEBULA

Remains of supernova

KINDBERG GALAXY (OK, I made that up. It's a tea stain.)

The light from distant stars takes so long to reach us that we're looking BACK in TIME.

Light from the CARINA NEBULA takes 8000 years to reach Earth, so we're looking at it as it was 8000 years ago, during our STONE AGE.

The HERSCHEL SPACE OBSERVATORY is the latest space telescope.

glint glint

telescope mirror 3.5m

It can orbit at around 1.5 million km from Earth.

Telescopes are useful, but it helps if you're a bit of a boffin too...

NEWTON

And Newton had some clever chums...

COMETS!

EDMOND HALLEY was a mate of Newton's.

Yes, in fact I persuaded him to publish his work—he'd kept quiet about it, for years!

Thanks, Ed!

He was also an astronomer.

I wrote a book about the southern stars.

In his spare time he made one of the first DIVING BELLS.

But he was most famous for...

COMETS are huge space snowballs made of ice, rock and metal.

As a comet travels closer to the Sun, it trails ice and dust behind it.

Comets orbit around the Sun in slightly WONKY paths.

Woe! woe!

I'm the ancient Greek ARISTOTLE.

Comets cause STRONG WINDS and DROUGHT!

(they don't)

Comets were seen as a sign of DISASTER (which isn't true either—unless you're a DINOSAUR...)

Urk

Halley used Newton's theories to work out that a particular comet returned close to the Earth at regular intervals.

Oh no!

It appeared just before the BATTLE of HASTINGS in 1066.

Halley spotted it in 1682...

Hmm... it has the same orbit as one that was last seen in 1607... it's the same one!

He didn't live to see it return as he'd predicted it would in 1758, by which time it had a name.

There goes Halley's Comet!

Some special comets...

When Halley's Comet passed by in 1910, comet-protecting UMBRELLAS and anti-comet PILLS went on sale.

I say!

Comet DONATI, seen in 1858, had 2 tails.

SHOEMAKER-LEVY 9 broke into bits and crashed into JUPITER in 1994.

HALE-BOPP, first seen in 1995, was especially big and bright.

Comet HYAKUTAKE had the longest tail ever — 570 million km (measured in 2000).

Comet-spotting became popular in the 1700s. Astronomer CAROLINE HERSCHEL discovered EIGHT of them.

There's another one!

One of them was named after her.

35P/HERSCHEL RIGOLLET

But Caroline wasn't as famous as her brother...

New Planets

WILLIAM HERSCHEL was a musician...

BOOMPA BOOMPA

and an astronomer in his spare time.

And he made telescopes, too...

It's a bit complicated, involves moulds using HORSE MANURE.

Pooh!

In 1781, with the help of his sister, the comet-hunter...

Ooh...I've discovered a new comet!

Another one?

YAWN

Hang on! It's not a comet, it's a new PLANET!

Yippee!

The other planets known about at this time (Mercury, Venus, Mars, Jupiter and Saturn) could all be seen with the naked eye.

After some debate, the new planet was called URANUS.

Uranus was the grandfather of Jupiter in classical mythology.

But I still prefer ROGER!

But as scientists delved further into space, our imaginations entered orbit as well...

SPACE STORIES

Back in 1668, MARGARET CAVENDISH wrote The Blazing World about a planet you can reach from the Arctic...

With some strange inhabitants,

Greetings, Parrot Man.

SQUARK!

Sss!

In a 1752 story by VOLTAIRE, a 120,000ft tall alien called MICROMEGAS...

travels to Earth on passing comets.

Hnn

In the space stories JULES VERNE wrote in the 1800s, three men are fired to the Moon by a cannon called Columbiad.

They orbit the Moon and make it back to Earth...

whey-hey!

without meeting any aliens (not so different from what happened in 1968).

There have been hundreds of SPACE MOVIES...
Not many of them feature friendly aliens...

And plenty of TV series too...

At the start of the 20th century
in a Swiss patents office...

EINSTEIN

Meanwhile...

SPEEDING GALAXIES

The biggest TELESCOPE in the world was built on top of MOUNT WILSON in California.

I'm MILTON HUMASON.

Hmm, this looks interesting.

Can I have a go?

Humason got a job as a cleaner at Mount Wilson.

But it turned out he was a brilliant astronomer.

What an amazing supernova!

He's a natural!

Hello there!

Scientist EDWIN HUBBLE came to work at Mount Wilson. Together, they made some amazing discoveries.

A few years before...

I'm VESTO MELVIN SLIPHER.

I observed other GALAXIES that seemed to be moving away from us.

And I'm HENRIETTA LEAVITT. I discovered interesting things about the brightness of STARS.

Thanks to them and other astronomers

...we worked out the distances of other galaxies

...and how fast they're moving.

WHOOSH!

Meanwhile, in a galaxy far, far away...

Hubble and Humason had revealed
the true vastness of the Universe.

But nobody knows much about planets in other solar systems within our own galaxy...let alone solar systems in other galaxies.

Hold on a bit, we're only just getting to know the ones in our own solar system.

The first planets outside our own solar system weren't discovered until 1992.

Hello, I'm ALEX WOLSZCZAN.

I found them!

300 or so planets have been proved to exist so far.

But within the visible Universe there are thought to be about 100 thousand million million million planets!

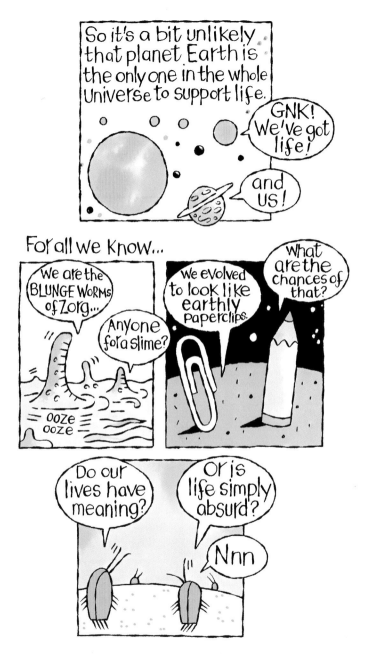

And if we don't know what they look like, how can we be sure they haven't arrived ALREADY...

CLOSE ENCOUNTERS

There have been thousands of reports of UFOs.

That's an UNIDENTIFIED FLYING OBJECT.

YIKES!

LONELY HILL

Some of them remain a MYSTERY, and some people think they are the aircraft of ALIEN BEINGS.

Yoo hoo, Earthling!

We mean you no harm.

Heh heh

The most famous UFO incident happened in New Mexico.

Nothing... unusual... here... at... all...

We recovered a weather balloon near ROSWELL.

Hnn

It's a government cover-up!

They really recovered a crashed alien spacecraft

...and the dead bodies of real aliens!

urk

PRESS

Since then, there have been many reports of differently shaped UFOs, like this...

Or this...

60

But the only way to find out what's really out there is to go and check…

SPACE RACE

To get out of Earth's atmosphere and into space, you need a rocket...

The first ones were made in CHINA 1000 years ago and used as weapons.

"Take that!"

WHOOSH

RUSSIAN scientist KONSTANTIN Tsiolkovsky was a rocket scientist

"Whoosh!"

"Whoosh!"

"One day the human race will colonise space, live for ever and become perfect."

But he didn't actually launch one.

ROBERT GODDARD launched the first LIQUID-FUEL rocket in 1926...

WHOOSH

"Wow... 12·5 metres"

Well, it was a start.

GERMAN V-2 rockets were launched in 1942 as weapons in the Second World War.

"Take that!"

WHOOSH

After the war, V-2s were developed for SPACE TRAVEL by a US team.

By this time, the two most powerful nations on Earth were the USA and USSR.

"Nng"

"Yes, and we don't get on."

"Nng"

They raced each other into space. SPUTNIK 1, the world's first ARTIFICIAL SATELLITE, was launched by the USSR in 1957.

"bleep bleep"

The following year, the first US satellite, EXPLORER 1, was launched.

"Whoosh"

"But we were first!"

But going back to the start of the race...

ANIMALS IN SPACE

Everyone was keen to get into space.

We can't wait!

But hang on a minute... we don't know the effects of weightlessness. How do we know people won't... EXPLODE or something?

Did she say 'explode'? GULP

Er... I'm feeling a bit less keen!

So the first living things weren't PEOPLE at all...

GULP

they were fruit flies.

Bzzz!

Whooshy

Since then many more animals have been sent beyond Earth's atmosphere—mostly monkeys, dogs and mice.

Nnng

Urrr

Squeeak

In 1957, LAIKA the dog was the first animal to orbit the Earth.

Urk

Laika didn't make it back to Earth.

STRELKA and BELKA were the first animals to go into orbit and come back alive.

Phew

But there have been some more unusual species too...

Croak

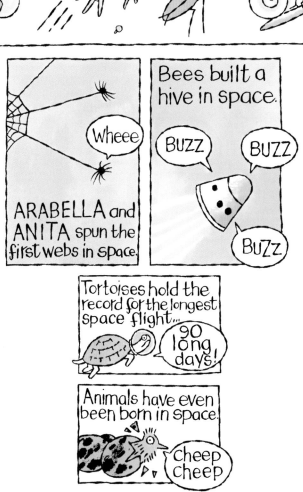

ARABELLA and ANITA spun the first webs in space.

Wheee

Bees built a hive in space.

BUZZ BUZZ BUZZ

Tortoises hold the record for the longest space flight...

90 long days!

Animals have even been born in space.

Cheep cheep

In 1961, the first PERSON went into space...

YURI GAGARIN

A 27-year-old Soviet pilot was about to become the most famous person on Earth...

I'm YURI!

Gosh!

On the way to the launch pad, Yuri had a pee (behind a bus). It's become a tradition for all Russian cosmonauts (at least, the male ones) ever since.

VOSTOK I blasted off into space on 12 April 1961.

Uh...it's a bit of a SQUEEZE!

Food and water for 10 days (just in case)

Yuri goes in here

Heat shield

2·3m

5m high

Huge rockets

GAGARIN entered Earth's orbit.

Wow... I'm the first person to see this ever!

Vostok I travelled at over 27000 Km/h, flying around the Earth in 89mins 34 secs.

The Americans were more determined than ever to win the next leg of the space race...

GRAVITY isn't as strong on the Moon as it is on Earth...

Wheee!

BUZZ ALDRIN was the second Moonwalker in the crew.

The astronauts took samples of lunar rock and dust, made notes and took photographs.

The American flag was planted on the Moon – it had to have a telescopic arm to make it fly without any wind.

Woof!

The landing was broadcast on TV – 500 million people watched.

There were 5 more Apollo missions and 10 more American astronauts walked on the Moon.

And because space was a brand new destination, people were desperate to do things FIRST...

Meanwhile, amazing discoveries were still being made...

Meanwhile, we sent animals... we sent people...
What could we send into space now?

SPACE PROBES

Sending PEOPLE into space is an awful lot of hassle.

You're telling ME!

SPACE PROBES are less bother. They don't get homesick and it doesn't matter if they're destroyed once they've finished their mission.

Tzzzt!

Tzzz

The first ones were sent to the Moon...

beepa beepa

This side is never seen from Earth

LUNA 3 gave us the first pictures of the far side of the Moon.

and Venus.

cccP

Some space probes fly past planets and send images back to Earth.

Dear Earth, Having a lovely time in space. Wish you were here.
Mariner 9 x

Oooh, look at that!

The Solar and Heliospheric Observatory (SOHO) has been observing the Sun since 1996.

MARS EXPLORATION ROVERS, Spirit and Opportunity, landed on Mars in 2004.

beepa beepa

and they're still sending us information.

PHOENIX is the most recent visitor to Mars.

Some space probes leave our Solar System and sail away into distant space.

Not shy!

Hang on, what's that?

PIONEER 10 and 11 began their long journey to JUPITER in the early seventies. They stopped transmitting to Earth but they're still out there somewhere.

In 1974, a radio message with information about humans was sent into space, beamed at a cluster of stars called M13.

YAWN

But it's so far away we'll have to wait about 50,000 years for a reply.

drum drum

VOYAGER 1 has travelled further from Earth than any other object made by humans.

16 billion km from the Sun

still transmitting to Earth

beepa beepa

Pioneer and Voyager carry MESSAGES in case they're found by ALIENS.

Gold-plated to protect against space dust

Greetings in 56 languages, 100 photos, binary code

And until we get one...

75

SPACE STATIONS

In 1971, the USSR launched the first ever space station.

SALYUT 1

We've been up here for ages.

In the 1970s and 80s, there was a series of new, improved SALYUTS.

Longer than the Americans!

Meanwhile, the USA launched its own space station.

SKYLAB (USA)

But...

How are we going to take people there and back?

Err, the SPACE SHUTTLE won't be ready until 1981!

NASA

So Skylab was abandoned in 1974. In 1979 it fell to Earth in Australia ... killing a cow.

URK

The USA decided to build a reusable aircraft instead of more space stations.

But what if you actually LIVED there?

LIVING IN SPACE

In some ways, living in space can be fun.

Whey-hey

Wheee

In others, it can be really annoying...

SUCK SUCK

Whoops!

My lunch is escaping!

Crumbs

Some astronauts suffer from space sickness...

GULP!

But they soon get used to life in space...

Sleeping...

Mm... cosy.

EYE MASK (there's no Earth night and day)

STRAPS (floating about while asleep can cause problems)

Eating...

Mmm... freeze-dried mince again!

LUNCH

DINNE

LUNCH

78

Exercising...

Astronauts on the first space stations came back to Earth very weak because there's no gravity to push against.

So we do lots of this to keep fit!

Going to the toilet...

Working...

Just off to do a few repairs...

in the terrifying emptiness of space.

Washing...

We try to avoid it as much as possible actually.

NASTY NIFF

And passing the time...

Floating tiddlywinks, anyone?

Not again!

Bet I can stay upside down the longest!

So, what's next?

We know what will happen on planet Earth in billions of years...

Earth

SUN

But will humans still be here?

Maybe we'll be able to recreate Earth conditions on other planets?

But what will happen to the rest of the Universe in the future?

Brr...

The Universe will spread out endlessly and get cooler – the BIG CHILL.

Crunch

OR the gravitational effect of all the matter in the Universe will be enough to reverse its expansion – the BIG CRUNCH.

But the expansion of the Universe is getting FASTER, because of DARK ENERGY!

We don't really know what dark energy is... but there's a lot of it.

Maybe, if dark energy continues to get stronger, everything will pull apart...

THE BIG RIP!

Will we ever make contact with intelligent life on other planets?

All over the world, people are listening...

to the furthest reaches of space...

beepa beepa

bleep bleep

tweeta tweet

cheep cheep

blip blop

beep

We're the SETI organisation...

the SEARCH for EXTRATERRESTRIAL INTELLIGENCE.

Yes!

We're listening for radio signals transmitted by ALIEN technology.

Perhaps one day we'll meet some...

Or perhaps, given the vastness of space and time, we never shall.

Tracey Turner

Tracey Turner writes books for children and adults about lots of different subjects, including famous writers, rude words, mysterious sliding rocks and, of course, the entire history of the Universe. When she's not travelling through space, she lives in Bath with Tom and their son, Toby.

Sally Kindberg

Sally Kindberg is an illustrator and writer. She once went to Elf School in Iceland, has written a book about hair, sailed on a tall ship to Lisbon and drawn the history of the world. She has one daughter, Emerald, and lives in London with 71 robots (and a couple of Moon rockets).

www.sallykindberg.co.uk

And for more Comic Strip History genius, don't miss ...